Fish
That Migrate

by Rufus Albermarle

 HOUGHTON MIFFLIN   BOSTON

ILLUSTRATION CREDIT: George Uhlrich

PHOTOGRAPHY CREDITS: Cover © Mark Conlin/SeaPics.com. 8-9 © VICTORIA MC CORMICK/Animals Animals-Earth Scenes. 12 © Chris Huss/SeaPics.com. 13 © Mark Conlin/SeaPics.com. 14 © Tim Watts.

Printed in China

ISBN-13: 978-0-547-01968-0

ISBN-10: 0-547-01968-8

7 8 9 0940 15 14 13
4500416911

Table of Contents

Introduction

Have you ever seen birds fly south in the fall? In some places, this lets you know that winter is coming. The birds are flying south to warmer places. This trip is called migration.

Lots of people know about bird migration. But not many people know that fish migrate, too! It's hard to see fish migrate, since fish travel through the water, not the air. But fish do migrate, even if we can't see them doing it!

Not all fish migrate. Some kinds of fish stay in the same home all year long. But other fish swim huge distances each year. Sometimes their trips are very dangerous. What makes some kinds of fish migrate?

Why Do Fish Migrate?

Fish migrate for the same reason birds do. They migrate for their survival. If they don't migrate, they will die.

Many fish migrate so they can find food. These fish may eat tiny plants and animals called plankton. Plankton lives in different places at different times of the year. So fish may travel a long way to find plankton to eat.

Fish migrate so that they can stay alive.

Fish try to lay their eggs in a place where the eggs won't be eaten.

Fish also migrate when they are going to lay eggs. Fish want to find the best place for their babies. Some baby fish don't eat the same foods that their parents eat. So the parents lay eggs where their babies will be able to find lots of food. Parent fish also lay eggs in safe places where the babies won't get eaten. Accidents like this don't happen as often if the parents migrate to a special place to lay their eggs.

Where Do Fish Migrate?

There are three main kinds of migrating fish.

The first kind of migrating fish is called oceanodromous (oh shu NOD reh mes). This kind of fish migrates only in the ocean, or salt water. Most fish that migrate are oceanodromous.

The second kind of migrating fish is called potamodromous (paw ta MOD reh mes). These fish migrate only in fresh water, such as rivers and streams.

The third kind of migrating fish is called diadromous (dye AD reh mes). These fish migrate between the ocean and fresh water. Diadromous fish may live in the ocean and migrate to a river when it's time to lay eggs. Or they may live in fresh water and then migrate to the ocean.

oceanodromous fish

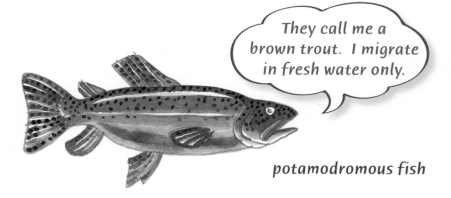

potamodromous fish

diadromous fish

There are three kinds of migrating fish.

Salmon swim up streams to lay their eggs.

Salmon are the most famous kind of migrating fish. Salmon are diadromous fish. They are born in fresh-water streams. Then they migrate to the ocean. The salmon live in the ocean for a few years. Then they swim back to the streams to lay their eggs.

salmon

When salmon migrate up a stream, it is a dramatic and amazing thing to see. The trip is very dangerous and can take three months. Salmon sometimes jump into the air, over powerful, thunderous waterfalls and through swirling waters, to get up a stream.

Some fish need a mix of fresh and salty water in their bodies.

From Fresh Water to Salt Water

Some fish that migrate have to be able to live in both fresh water and salt water. How do they do it?

Fish that live in fresh water have plenty of salt in their bodies. But too much salt is not good for them. So, when these fish swim, their skin absorbs, or takes in, fresh water. The water mixes with the salt. So these fish always have the right mix of fresh water and salt water in their bodies.

When fish that live in fresh water migrate to salt water, they have to do something different. The fish will drink salt water to keep their bodies from drying out. Then their bodies get rid of the extra salt, so the fish keep the right mix of fresh water and salty water in their bodies.

Only a few kinds of fish can live in both fresh and salt water. These fish include salmon and some kinds of trout and herring.

Fresh Water to Salt Water

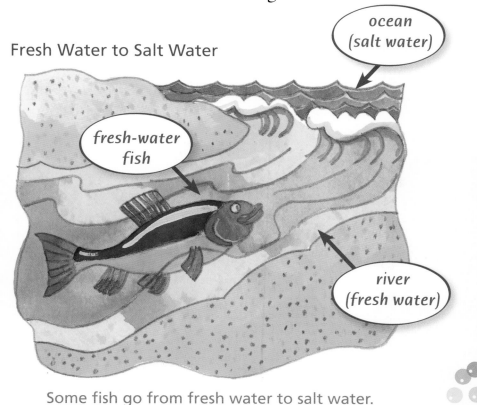

Some fish go from fresh water to salt water.

How Do Fish Know Where to Go?

How do fish know where to go when they migrate?

Some fish use smell to tell them which way to go in the underwater landscape. Smell tells salmon how to get from the ocean to fresh water, and then back again. Each salmon remembers the smell of the stream where it was born. When the salmon grows up, it migrates from the ocean back to that stream. Some salmon travel thousands of miles to get to the streams. The stream's smell gets stronger as the salmon gets closer to it.

Salmon use smell to help them migrate.

Ahh.
The sweet smell of
fresh water!

salmon

12

We tuna follow the changes in the ocean temperature.

tuna

Tuna use water temperature to help them migrate.

But fish don't always use smell to migrate. Some fish use the temperature of the water to guide them. If the water gets too chilly or too warm, the fish may know they aren't going the right way.

Scientists don't know how all fish migrate. Some eels migrate almost 4,000 miles to the place where they lay eggs. These eels even wiggle over dry land and solid objects, such as pipes, when they migrate. But scientists are not sure how eels know which way to go.

Eels face many frightening dangers on their trip. But eels don't think about that. Like all migrating fish, they just keep swimming!

Eels migrate through or over almost anything.

eels

Nothing can stop EEL MIGRATION!

Responding

Compare and Contrast

Copy the chart below. Complete the chart by writing one detail about what each fish does that the other does not.

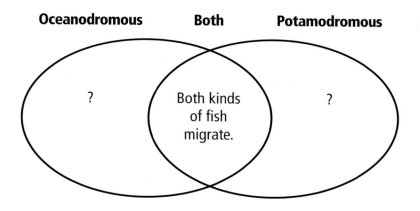

Oceanodromous **Both** **Potamodromous**

? | Both kinds of fish migrate. | ?

Write About It

Text to World What if suddenly there were no more fish? Write a paragraph describing what the world would be like. What would be the same? What would be different?

accidents	migrate
chilly	plenty
dramatic	solid
frightening	survival
landscape	thunderous

TARGET SKILL **Compare and Contrast** Tell how details or ideas are alike and different.

TARGET STRATEGY **Visualize** As you read, use selection details to picture what is happening.

GENRE **Informational text** gives factual information about a topic.